Pilgrim Children Had Many Chores

Pilgrim children had many chores.
They had to churn butter.

They had to muck the garden.

They had to tie wheat into bundles.

They had to get water from the well. 5

They had to feed chickens.

They had to gather firewood.

They had to serve meals, too!